An aid to communication on Tyneside and thereabouts

Devised, compiled, designed and illustrated by George Todd

ISBN-10 0-946928-09-6
ISBN-13 978-0-946928-09-5
This edition 2001, this reprint 2020
Originally published by Frank Graham
Published by Butler Publishing in 1987

© 1987 Butler Publishing, Thropton, Morpeth,
Northumberland NE65 7LP

This booklet is laid out in two columns per page. In the
left-hand column the dialect word or phrase is set in bold
type and directly underneath, the context in which it might
be used. In the right-hand column is the translation.

Butler
publishing

What is a Geordie?

There is dissension, even in our own ranks, over a precise definition of the title. Is he a Tynesider? That is to say, was he born on the banks of the Tyne? And if so, where do the boundaries of the banks lie? Is he a native of Northumberland or of Durham or of both? Is he discernible, as some to the south would have it, as an idle, beer-sodden, wife-beating savage? Or is he, as some north of the border incessantly claim, a Scotsman with his brains kicked out? A particularly ungrateful observation considering that our wall * offered them protection from the Romans.

So what *is* a Geordie?

I have met men as far removed from the Tyne as Darlington to the south and Berwick to the north who did not demur when regarded as Geordie. And yet there are those born and bred in Newcastle and the immediate vicinity to whom the term 'Geordie', when applied to them, is anathema. It seems to me that just as class discrimination perpetuates by voluntary subscription, so does the Geordie identity. "I believe, therefore I am." A Geordie is one who regards himself as such and as far as I am concerned, all recruits are welcome.

There is, of course, the language barrier, a serious problem for a novice Geordie.

This phrase book has been compiled to assist novices and visitors to assimilate themselves and to act as a refresher for lapsed Geordies. It comprises words and phrases culled from conversations with old friends and relations, various printed works (some of them quite ancient) and from my own experience, man and boy, on Tyneside. Some readers will find my definitions to be at variance with their own. I can only plead that just as vowel sounds vary from place to place, sometimes only a few miles apart, so do certain word meanings. Finally, with regard to vowel sounds and general pronunciation, I have left it to the reader to rely on day to day experience. Getting the phonetics right will take a better man than I am.

* As in many historical issues the mists of time have served to hide the truth and to send historians in the wrong direction. The popular view that the wall was built by Hadrian to keep out the Scots is erroneous. It was, in fact, erected to keep the Romans at bay by a Northumbrian builder of the period by the similar name of Adrian Leech. Cockney mercenaries in the Roman force travelling home on leave talked, in awe, of "Adrian's wall", and because of the well known Cockney practice of dropping the 'h' it was generally assumed that they meant "Hadrian's Wall".

George Todd, December 1, 1976

argyin' the toss

Aa
Aa divvin' knaa

I
I do not know

aa'
Thor aa' gyen

all
They are all gone

aad
Canny aad sowl

old
Nice old soul

Aa'd
Aa'd better gan canny

I had
I had better be careful

Aa'd
Aa'd fettle hor

I would
*I would put a stop to her
(tantrums)*

aaful
Me throat's aaful gyezend

awful
*My throat is awfully
parched*

aah
Aah, but Aa is!

oh
Oh, but I am!

aakwaad
Thon's ganna be aakwaad

awkward
*That is going to be
awkward*

aakwaad

He's an aakwaad nowt

obstreperous, deliberately
difficult (person)
*He is a difficult person of
no importance*

aal
Aal ower

all
All over

aalreet
Aalreet whey?

alright
Alright then?

aan
It's me aan

own
It is my own

Aa've
Aa've dyun

I have
I have finished

Aa waarned
*Ye'll be gannin ti the toon
Aa waarned?*

I suppose
*You are going to Newcastle
I suppose?*

3

aback
He's aback o' wi

behind
He is behind us

aback o' the fire

Hoy it aback o' the fire

on the domestic fire
(kitchen range)
Throw it on the fire

aboot
Wor aboot paid

about
We are about exhausted

abyun
Up abyun i' the loft

above
Up above in the loft

actin' horsell/he'ssell
She's elwis actin' horsell

whining; protesting
She is always protesting

afear'd
Thor's nowt to be afear'd on

afraid
There is nothing to be afraid of

a few broth
D'ye waant a few broth, hinny?

some broth
Do you want some broth, love?

afore
Afore the morn

before
Before tomorrow

agyen
Dee it agyen

again
Do it again

agyen't
Aa'm agyen't

against it
I am against it

ahaad
Tyek ahaad o' thon

hold
Take hold of that

aheyte
Hoy the baal up aheyte

in the air
Throw the ball in the air

ahint
He's ahint o' wi

behind
He is behind us

airm
Aa've hort me airm

arm
I have hurt my arm

alang
Gan alang thonder

along
Go along yonder

alen
Leave is alen

alone
Leave me alone

amangst
Amangst aal o' wi

amongst
Amongst all of us

4

answers
Aa'm all clear as far as the morn neet answers

is concerned
I am free as far as tomorrow night is concerned

any amoont
Aa've got any amoont o' tetties

plenty
I have plenty of potatoes

argie
Divvint argie wiv hor

argue
Do not argue with her

argyin' the toss
Thor argyin' the toss agyen

in dispute
They are in dispute again

arly
Divvin' forget ti lowp up arly the morn

early
Do not forget to rise early tomorrow

arn
Aa divvint arn enyuf

earn
I do not earn enough

atween
Thor's nowt atween them

between
There is nothing between them

ax
Ax wor lass

ask
Ask my wife

bummlor

baaldy pyet

baad
He's varry baad

ill
He is very ill

baadly-liked
He's varry baadly-liked

disliked
He is much disliked

baal
Haddaway an' stott yor baal

ball
Go and bounce your ball

babby
Tyek ahaad o' the babby a min't

baby
Take hold of the baby a minute

baff weekend

the weekend without pay when miners were paid fortnightly

Aa had nowt left bi baff weekend

I had nothing left by baff weekend

5

bairn
Thor nowt but bairns

baby or small child
They are merely children

bait
Whaat hae ye got for yor bait, mar?

food carried to work
What do you have to eat, mate?

bait-poke
Aa've forgettin me bait-poke

food-bag carried to work
I have forgotten my food-bag

banked up
She's weel banked up

piled up
The coal on the fire is well piled up

bargie
Aa bargie thon kyek

claim
I claim that cake

barry
Wor ganna barry him the morn

bury
We are going to bury him tomorrow

bar them

How! Bar them!

halt the proceedings (at a pitch and toss school)
Hey! Stop!

bat
Aa got a bat i' the fyess

blow
I got a blow in the face

begox
Begox, ye gi's a aaful gliff

by God
By God, you gave me an awful fright

belly-timmor
Aa could dee wi' some belly-timmor

food
I am hungry

bi
Doon bi the wettor

by
Down by the river

bi'd
Aa was tyun in bi'd

by it
I was fooled by it

bide
Bide heor

wait
Wait here

bile
Me bile's borst

boil
My boil has burst

bit's o' bairns
Thor nowt but bits o' bairns

children
They are but children

biv
He's biv he'ssell

by
He is alone

blaa
Blaa the lowe oot
blow
Blow out the light

blaa
Haad on till Aa get me blaa
breath
Wait until I get my breath back

blaa
Gi's a blaa whey?
a puff from a cigarette
Give me a puff then?

blaan-oot
Aa'm fair blaan-oot
blown-out
I have eaten too much food

blackclock
The nettie's liftin' wi blackclocks
cockroach
The lavatory is full of cockroaches

blair
Whaat's he blairin' aboot?
cry
Why is he crying?

bleachin'
It's bleachin' doon ootside
heavy/driving (rain)
It is stormy outside

bleezor
Put the bleezor on till it tyeks ahaad
fire blazer
Use the blazer until the fire takes hold

blethor
He's full o' nowt but blethor
aimless talk
He talks aimlessly

blethorskite
He's an aaful blethorskite
one who talks aimlessly
He is full of worthless nonsense

blogged
The spoot's blogged
blocked
The spout is blocked

body
She's a canny aad body
person
She is a nice old person

bogie
Len's yor bogie?
a four-wheeled trolley or two-wheeled barrow
Lend me your barrow?

bone
Aa'll bone him aboot thon
interrogate
I will question him about that matter

bonny
She's a bonny lass
pretty; handsome
She is a pretty girl

bonny
He's a bonny footbaaller
accomplished
He is an accomplished footballer

7

bonny an' baad
Me faathor's bonny an' baad

very ill
My father is very ill

bonny an' clivvor
Wor bairn's bonny an' clivvor

very clever
Our child is very clever

bonny lad
Noo then, bonny lad

friend; mate
Hello, mate.

bonny on
Wor bonny on noo

in trouble
We are in trouble now

bool
Whee's ganna bool forst?

bowl
Who is going to bowl first?

bools
Howway hinny, Aa'll play ye at bools

bowls
Come on mate, I will play you at bowls

boonds
Oot o'boonds

bounds
Out of bounds

boot
Aa've had a baad boot o' flu

bout
I have had a bad bout of flu

bord
Is thon bord a spuggy?

bird
Is that bird a sparrow?

borst
Me baal's borst

burst
My ball is burst

bowk
Divvin' bowk see much

belch
Do not belch so much

bowld
Here's the bowld laad he'ssell

bold
Here is the bold boy himself

bowt
Aa've bowt mesell some new claes

bought
I have bought myself some new clothes

bray
Aa'll bray ye

thrash
I will thrash you

breed
Is thor nee breed, Maam?

bread
Is there no bread, Mother?

breeks
Is them yor aad breeks?

trousers
Are they your old trousers?

breeth
Aa canna get me breeth

breath
I cannot breath

brickfist
Whaat's for brickfist the morn?

breakfast
What is for breakfast tomorrow

brokken
Me gully's brokken

broken
My knife has broken

broon
Broon byuts

brown
Brown boots

browt
Aa've browt a marra o' yors

brought
I have brought a friend of yours

browtin's up
Noo, mind your browtin's up

upbringing
Now, remember your upbringing

bubble
Give ower bubblin'

cry
Stop crying

bullet
Gi's a bullet whey?

a sweet
Give me a sweet then?

bummlor
Waatch oot, theors a bummlor

bee
Look out, there is a bee

bumpor
Gi's yor bumpor

glass or pot
Hand me your glass

bump the set
He'll bump the set syun

get into trouble
He will be in trouble soon

byek
Byek wi some stotty kyek

bake
Bake us some stotty cake

byeth
Thor byeth deef

both
They are both deaf

byut
Aa'll gi ye a byut i' the hintend

boot
I will kick your posterior

crackett

cuttie

caad
It's a caad neet the neet

cold
It is cold tonight

9

caadriffe
Aa feel aal caadriffe

shivery
I feel very shivery

caal
Gi's a caal the morn

call
Give me a call tomorrow

caase
Whaat's the caase on't?

cause
What is causing it?

cairt
Hoy'd o' the cairt

cart
Throw it on the cart

cakky
*Mind ye divvint stamp i'
thon cakky*

animal or human waste
*Make sure you avoid
treading in that waste*

canna
Aa canna dee it

cannot
I cannot do it

canny
He's a canny laad

nice
He is a nice boy

canny
Gan canny

careful
Be careful

canny
Canny on

steady
Steady on

canny
It's canny

average; alright
It's alright

canny-crack
He's a canny-crack

glib
He is glib

carlins

*Ower many carlins blaa ye
oot*

black-coated peas eaten
boiled or raw
*Too many carlins give you
wind*

champion
It's champion, mar

first-class
It is first-class, mate

chare
Dee away up thon chare

narrow lane or alley
Go up that alley

chep
Canny aad chep

chap
Nice old chap

cheyn
A waatch an' cheyn

chain
A watch and chain

chimli
*Canny on or ye'll set the
chimli ahaad*

chimney
*Steady on or you will set
the chimney on fire*

chorch
He's a reglor chorchgannor

church
He is a regular churchgoer

chow
Gi's a chow whey?

chew
*Give me a chew (of
tobacco) then?*

chowk
Aa varnigh chowked mesell

choke
I nearly choked myself

claes
Me woork claes

clothes
My working clothes

clag
He'll clag ye

hit
He will hit you

clag
Clag a stamp on't

stick
Stick a stamp on it

claggum
Gi's the claggum

glue
Give me the glue

claggy
It's aaful claggy

sticky
It is awfully sticky

clartin' aboot
Give ower clartin' aboot

messing about
Stop messing about

clarts
Bide oot the clarts

mud
Stay out of the mud

clarty
It's varry clarty

muddy
It is very muddy

clarty
A clarty affair

cheap and nasty
A cheap and nasty item

clash
*Divvin' clash the door
aback o' ye*

slam
*Do not slam the door
behind you*

clip

unorthodox or untidy
dresser
He is a mess
He's a proper clip

clip
Aa'll clip yor lug

strike
I will strike your ear

clivvor
He's bonny an' clivvor

clever
He is very clever

clivvor
She's not ower clivvor

well
She is unwell

11

clood
It's cloody ower thonder

cloud
It is cloudy over there

cloon
He's a daft cloon

clown
He is a silly clown

cloot
Hae ye an aad cloot?

cloth
Have you an old cloth?

cloot
Gi'd a cloot

strike
Strike it

cocked he's/hor toes up
She's nivver been the syem since Geordie cocked he's toes up

died
She has never been the same since Geordie died

cockle
Divvin' cockle o' the grund

spit
Do not spit on the ground

coin
Coin oot the way afore wi dunsh

turn
Turn aside or we will crash

collry
He woorks at the collry

colliery
He works at the colliery

come-bye
Howway, come-bye!

get out of the way
Come on, get out of the way!

comin' on amain
Me leeks is comin' on amain

doing very well
My leeks are doing very well

coo
Lukka thon coo

cow
Look at that cow

cooch
Sit ye doon o' the cooch

couch
Sit down on the couch

coonty
He plays bools for the coonty

county
He plays bowls for the county

corl
A corly-heeded bairn

curl
A curly-headed baby

cottrills
Hoo are ye off for cottrills?

cash; money
Do you have any money?

could'nt shoot coal
He could'nt shoot coal

cannot sing
He cannot sing

cowie
Aa divvin' like boolin' tiv a cowie

left-handed batsman
I do not like bowling to a left-hander

cowp
Be canny or ye'll cowp it

spill
Be careful or you will spill it

cowp
Aa'll cowp ye

swop
I will swop you

cowped he's/hor creels
He tripped ower an' cowped he's creels

somersaulted
He tripped and somersaulted

cowpin' he's/hor boilie
He's cowpin' he's boilie i' the nettie

being sick
He is being sick in the lavatory

crack
Howway in for a bit crack

conversation; chat
Come inside for a chat

crackett
Plank yorsell doon o' thon crackett

small wooden stool
Sit down on that stool

cree
Aa'm ganna fettle up a chicken cree

coop
I am going to make a chicken coop

cuddy
Lowp o' yor cuddy

horse
Leap on to your horse

cue
He's iv a bad cue wiv he'ssell

mood
He is in a bad mood

cuttie
He's bi the fire wiv a cuttie

short pipe
He is smoking his pipe by the fire

cyuk
She canna cyuk

cook
She cannot cook

dut

daad
Gi'd a daad wi the mell

strike
Strike it with the sledgehammer

dash

Get's a dash

drink made from a mixture of beer and lemonade
Get me a dash

13

dee
Dee away wi'd

do
Do away with it

dee away
Dee away whey

make a start
Make a start then

deed
He's deed

dead
He is dead

deein' he's/hor dickors

*Cassius Clay's been deein'
he's dickors agyen*

performing acrobatics/
dance
*Cassius Clay has been
clowning again*

deef
*Ye'll hae to shoot 'cos he's
deef*

deaf
*You will have to shout
because he is deaf*

demmed
The bar's demmed

full to capacity
The bar is full up

di'd
Aa didn't di'd

do it
I did not do it

div
Div Aa knea him?

do
Do I know him?

divvint
Aa divvint mind o' thon

do not
I do not remember that

Dode
Wor Dode

George
Our George

dollar
*Are ye ganna len's a
dollar?*

five shillings (25p)
Will you lend me 25p ?

dook
*Dook yor heed for thon
timmor*

duck
*Duck your head to avoid
that beam*

doon
Aa'm gannin' doon the raa

down
I am going down the street

doon-bye
Are ye gannin' doon-bye?

down there
Are you going down there?

doot
Nee doot aboot it

doubt
No doubt about it

dor
*Dor ye lowp ower thon
yett?*

dare
*Dare you leap over that
gate?*

dorna
A dorna dee it

dare not
I dare not do it

dorsent
He dorsent show he's fyess

dare not
He dare not show his face

dorty
Me claes is dorty

dirty
My clothes are dirty

dose o' caad
Aa've gettin a dose o' caad

bout of cold/flu
I have caught flu

dotherin
*Whaat are ye dotherin'
aboot for?*

acting uncertainly
*Why are you acting
uncertainly?*

dottin' aboot
*Aa've seen him dottin'
aboot*

casual movement
*I have seen him about the
place*

double neif
Aa'll gi ye me double neif

fist
I will punch you

dowter
*He's dowter tyeks care on
him*

daughter
*His daughter takes care of
him*

dozzent
He's dozzent

slow, stupid
He is stupid

draa
Draa's a pictor?

draw
Draw me a picture?

droon
Divvin' droon yorsell

drown
Do not drown yourself

droonded
He droonded he'sell

drowned
He drowned himself

droothy

He was aaful droothy

thirsty; a taste for an
excess of strong drink
He drank a lot

duff
Hoy some duff ower the fire

coarse coal dust
Put some duff on the fire

dump
Gi's yor dump

cigarette butt
Give me your fag end

dunsh
*Be canny or we'll dunsh
summick*

crash
*Be careful or we will crash
into something*

dut
He elwis had a dut iv he's heed

bowler hat
He always had a bowler hat on his head

duzzy
Aa've gyen aal duzzy

dizzy
I have gone very dizzy

dyun
Aa'm dyun wi'd

done
I am done with it

eftor
Whaat are ye eftor?

after
What are you after?

elwis
He's elwis wrang

always
He is always wrong

empy
Me pockets is empy

empty
My pockets are empty

enyuf
Haad on, that's enyuf

enough
Hold on, that is enough

ettle
Aa ettled that was ganna happen

expect
I expected that to happen

fadge
Aa like nowt bettor than a fadge

a flat bread loaf
I like nothing better than a fadge

fair-beat
He's fair-beat

worn out
He is worn out

fairin
Is thon a fairin for Jinny?

a lover's present
Is that a present for Jean?

fash
Divvint fash yorsell for me

trouble
Do not trouble yourself for me

fear'd
Are ye fear'd on't?

frightened
Are you frightened of it?

femmur
It's ower femmur

fragile
It is too fragile

fettle
He's in baad fettle

condition
He is in a poor condition

fettle
Can ye fettle it up?

fix
Can you fix it up?

fettle
Can ye fettle wi up a crackett?

make
Can you make us a stool?

fettle
He's iv a baad fettle wiv he'sell

mood
He is in a bad mood

fettle
Aa'll fettle him

put a stop to
I will put a stop to him

fillum
Aa seen a good fillum last neet

film
I saw a good film last night

findin' aboot
Whaat are ye findin' aboot doon theor for?

searching
What are you searching for down there

fit as a lop
He's lowpin' aboot, fit as a lop

fit as a flea
He is jumping about a fit as a flea

flannins
It's caad enyuf for yor flannins

flannel underwear
It's cold enough for your flannel underwear

flap
Yor flap's oppen

trouser fly
Your fly is open

fleein
Thor's a haak fleein' aboot

flying
There is a hawk flying about

floo-ors
Lukka them bonny floo-ors

flowers
Look at those pretty flowers

foisty
It's foisty in-bye

damp and smelly
It is damp and smelly in there

fond
He's dyun some fond things iv he's time

silly
He has done some silly things in his time

footbaal
Howway, wor ganna play footbaal

football
Come on, we are going to play football

footrunner
Ye hae ti waatch them footrunners

professional sprinter
You must not trust professional sprinters

for'd
Waatch oot for'd

for it
Look out for it

forebye
Forebye thon ye'll hae ti fettle this up

as well as
As well as that you will have to fix this

for fairs
He's gannin' for fairs noo

with serious intent
He is now trying seriously

forkytail
Thor's forkytails i' the floo-ors

earwig
There are earwigs in the flowers

fornenst
Divvint lean fornenst the yett

against; in front of
Do not lean against the gate

forst
Aa won forst ower

first
I won first time

fower
Fower an' fower myeks eyht

four
Four and four makes eight

fowt
He fowt weel

fought
He fought well

frae
He's frae the toon

from
He is from Newcastle

front-room
Howway inti the front-room

lounge
Come into the lounge

frozzin
Aa'm varnigh frozzin

frozen
I am nearly frozen

fuddled
She fuddled wiv him last neet

cuddled
She cuddled with him last night

fund
Aa've fund a pund

found
I have found a pound

funnin'
Aa was only funnin'

joking
I was only joking

fyess
Mind ye divvin' get a bat o' the fyess

face
Be careful not to get hit in the face

fyessy
She's a fyessy bitch

cheeky; brazen
She is a brazen woman

fyul
Haddaway ye aad fyul

fool
Go away you old fool

fyullin'
Give ower fyullin'

fooling about
Stop fooling about

gaak
Whaat are ye gaakin' at?

stare
What are you staring at?

gadgie
Whee's the gadgie

old man
Who is the old man?

gaffe
Are ye gannin' to the gaffe?

cinema
Are you going to the
cinema?

gaffor
Aa's the gaffor heor

boss
I am the boss here

gallisses
Me gallisses is snapped

trouser braces
My braces have snapped

gallowa
*He eats enyuff for a
gallowa*

horse
He eats like a horse

gammlin'
*He's far ower fond o'
gammlin'*

gambling
He gambles too much

gan
Gan canny

go
Go easy

gannin'
Are ye gannin' hyem?

going
Are you going home?

gannin' he's/hor ends
*Jonty's gannin' he's ends
oot theor*

shouting excitedly
John is creating a fuss out
there

gannon
Gannon whey

go on
Go on then

ganny
Aa hev a canny aad ganny

grandmother
I have a nice old
grandmother

gan-on
Whaat an aaful gan-on

fuss
What an awful fuss

19

gan-on
Hoo de ye gan-on?

procedure
What is the procedure?

ganzie
Haad on till Aa get me ganzie off

jersey
Wait until I remove my jersey

geet
Geet big gob

great
Great big mouth

Geordie
Noo then, Geordie

George
Hello, George

gettin
Aa've gettin some new byuts

got
I have got some new boots

gettin away
Aad Bill's gettin away

dead
Old Bill is dead

gi'
Gi's a tab

give
Give me a cigarette

gill
Aa'll just hev a gill

half-pint of beer
I will have just a half-pint

gissie
Howway see the gissies

pig
Come and see the pigs

give ower
Give ower howkin' yor sneck

stop
Stop picking your nose

glaky
He's a bit glaky

slow witted
He is a bit slow

gliff
He gi's an aaful gliff

fright
He gave me an awful fright

glower
Divvin' glower at me

glare
Do not glare at me

gollup
Ye sharp golluped thon doon

gulp; eat quickly
You ate that quickly

gord

Haddaway an' bool yor gord

iron/metal hoop propelled and controlled by a metal hook
Go and bowl your hoop

gowk
Hoy yor gowk o' the fire

apple core
Throw your apple core on the fire

grafflin'

Aa was grafflin' aboot i' the dark

searching for something with the hand
I was searching in the darkness

greet
A greet big chep

great
A great big man

gripe
Gi's thon gripe

garden fork
Give me that garden fork

grund
The grund's ower clarty

ground
The ground is too muddy

guisors

The guisors is comin' doon the raa

pit lane revellers in fancy dress
The revellers are coming down the lane

gully
Be canny wi thon gully

large knife
Be careful with that knife

gyen
Hes he gyen hyem?

gone
Has he gone home?

gyen all to smaal
He's gyen aal to smaal

gone to pieces
He has gone to pieces

gyep
Whaat are ye gyeppin' at?

gape
What are you gaping at?

Gyetsid
Aa'm gannin' to Gyetsid

Gateshead
I am going to Gateshead

gyezend
Gi's a pint, Aa'm gyezend

parched
Give me a pint, I am parched

haad
Tyek a haad on't

hold
Take hold of it

haad on
Haad on a min't

hold on
Hold on a minute

haad yor whisht
Haad yor whisht for five, man!

hold your tongue
Hold your tongue for five minutes, man!

hoyin' up

haaf
Aa'll be back hyem in haaf an hoor

half
I will be back home in half an hour

haak
Haak it up heor

pull
Pull it up here

haaker
The haaker can tyek it

hawker
The hawker can take it

hacky
Divvin' be see hacky

dirty
Do not be so dirty

hacky-dorty
Whey, it's hacky-dorty!

very dirty
Well, it's very dirty!

haddaway
Haddaway an' get the clarts off ye

go away
Go away and clean the mud off yourself

hae
Hae ye got owt for the bairn?

have
Have you got anything for the baby?

hae'd
Ye canna hae'd

have it
You cannot have it

hang fire
Hang fire a mow

wait
Wait a moment

hap
Hap yorsell weel up agyen the cad

wrap
Wrap yourself up well against the cold

hap-past
Aa'll see ye doon-bye at hap-past

half-past
I will meet you down there at half-past

hard
Aa nivvor hard

heard
I never heard

hard card
Aa'm o' the hard card

penury
I have no money

heed
He got a bat o' the heed

head
He was hit on the head

help
Help this (beer glass) agyen

fill
Fill this again

heor
Hoo are wi deein' heor, mar?

here
How are we doing here, mate?

he'ssell
He's not ower clivvor he'ssell

himself
He himself is not too well

het
It was see het it bornd is

hot
It was so hot that it burnt me

hev
Hev ye dyun?

have
Have you finished?

hey-up!
Hey-up! Thor's a chep waantin' past

look out!
Look out! A man wants to be past

hing
Hing yor claes up o' the hyuk

hang
Hang your clothes up on the hook

hinny

Hoo are ye gaan-on, hinny?

expression of endearment of indeterminate meaning
How are you getting on, hinny?

hintend
Aa'll tyek me byut ti yor hintend

posterior
I will kick your posterior

hippins
Aa'm just ganna wesh the bairn's hippins oot

nappies
I am just going to wash the baby's nappies

hippy-lazy
She winnit de it 'cos she's hippy-lazy

idle
She will not do it because she is idle

hit
This is hit heor

it
This is it here

honkers
Sittin' doon iv he's honkers

haunches
Sitting on his haunches

hoo
Hoo do ye dee thon?

how
How do you do that?

hooky
He's been playin' hooky agyen

truancy
He has been playing truant again

hooky-mat

Aa'm myekkin' a hooky-mat

a mat made from sacking and rags
I am making a hooky-mat

hoose
Wor hoose is bornt doon

house
Our house has burnt down

hoppins
Wor gannin to the hoppins

a fair
We are going to the fair

horsell
She's biv horsell

herself
She is by herself

how!
How! Yee!

hey!
Hey! You!

howk
Aa'll howk ye

belabour
I will belabour you

howk
Divvint howk yor sneck

pick; dig
Do not pick your nose

howld
Tyek a howld on't

hold
Take hold of it

howway
Howway hyem

come on
Come on home

hoy
Hoy'd ower

throw
Throw it over

hoy'd he's/hor hand in
The aad chep's hoy'd he's hand in

given up
The old man has given up

hoyer-oot
Thon geet big chep must be the hoyer-oot

thrower-out
That big man must be the thrower-out

hoyin' oot time
Howway laads, it's hoyin' oot time

closing time
Come on boys, it is closing time

hoyin' skyul
He's a keekor for the hoyin' skyul

pitch-and-toss gathering
He is a look-out for the pitch-and-toss players

hoyin' up

Whee's hoyin' up?

the throwing up of coins in pitch-and-toss
Who is throwing up the coins?

hoy-oot

Howway laads, thor's a hoy-oot

the throwing out of coins from a wedding car
Come on boys, there is a hoy-oot

hoy the dreg in
Wah gannin ower fast, hoy the dreg in

stop it (pit tub)
We are going too fast, stop it

hump
Hump it ower heor

carry
Carry it over here

hyem
Wor lass is at hyem

home
My wife is at home

hyuk
Hae ye got hor hyukked up?

hook
Is it hooked up?

impittent
Ye impittent little yep

impertinent
You cheeky little ape/ monkey

in-back
Aa'm in-back next week

in day shift at the colliery
I am working day shift next week

in-bye
Are ye gannin' in-bye?

in there
Are you going in there?

in-forst
Aa'm in-forst the morn

in first shift at the colliery
I am in first shift tomorrow

inti'd
He lowped inti'd

into it
He jumped into it

intiv
Aa've looked intiv it

into
I have looked into it

is
Pass is the gully

me
Pass me the knife

isteed
He'll dee owt insteed o' woork

instead
He will do anything instead of work

iv
He geans aboot iv a cairt

in
He goes about in a cart

iv
Lowp iv a bus

on
Jump on a bus

ivvor
Be ivvor see canny

ever
Be ever so careful

jaapin

An Easter game where hard-boiled eggs are knocked one against another to see which is first to crack

Howway, Aa'll jaap ye
Come on, I will jaap you

Jarmin
Aa've gettin Jarmin measles

German
I have German measles

jarsie
Thon jarsie's a bobbydazzlor

jersey
That jersey is brightly coloured

Jonty
Wor Jonty

John
Our John

jorms
Divvint spread yor jorms ower heor

germs
Do not spread your germs over here

keek
Hae yoursell a keek at thon

look
Have a look at that

keekor
Whee's ganna be keekor?

look-out
Who is going to be look-out?

keep-ahaad
Keep ahaad whey

take care of yourself
Take care of yourself then

ken
Aa ken him weel

know
I know him well

ken
Do you ken the aad raas?

remember
Do you remember the old streets?

kep
Kep the baal

catch
Catch the ball

kitchen
Howway into the kitchen, hinny

dining room
Come into the dining room, pet

kite
Wiv a kite like thon he canna see he's byuts

large stomach
With a large stomach like that he cannot see his shoes

kittle
Divvint kittle is

tickle
Do not tickle me

knaa
Ye knaa fine weel

know
You know quite well

knakky-kneed
He's ower knakky-kneed

knock-kneed
He is too knock-kneed

krutt
He's got a baaldy krutt

head
He has a bald head

kyek
Gi's a bit o' kyek

cake
Give me a piece of cake

kyel
The kyel's ready

soup; broth
The soup is ready

lace
Dee what yor telt or Aa'll lace ye

thrash
Do what you are told or I will thrash you

lakky
Aa want some lakky for me 'pult

elastic
I want some elastic for my catapult

lang
Them days is lang gyen

long
Those days are long gone

larn
Aa'll larn ye

teach
I will teach you

lassie
A bonny lassie

girl
A pretty girl

lavvy
Whee's i' the lavvy?

lavatory
Who is in the lavatory?

lavvy-paan
Pour it doon the lavvy-pan

lavatory-pan
Pour it into the lavatory-pan

let
The spuggy's let intiv a tree

alighted
The sparrow has alighted into a tree

liftin'
It's liftin' wi forkytails

full of
It is full of earwigs

linin's
Hae ye got some clean linin's for's?

underpants
Do you have clean underpants for me?

lintie
He's lowpin' about like a lintie

linnet
He is hopping about like a linnet

lonnen
Gan reet doon this lonnen

long straight road
Go right down this long straight road

loopy
She's ganna hae's loopy

insane
She is going to have me insane

lop
Fit as a lop

flea
Fit as a flea

lowe
Put thon lowe ower heor

light
Shine the light over here

lowp
Lowp on, mar

jump
Jump on, mate

lowpin' up an' doon
He's lowpin' up an' doon ower nowt

a state of excitement
He is excited over nothing

lowse
Howway laads, it's lowse

finishing time; closing time
Come on boys, it is closing time

lowse
Lowse me byuts, hinny

loosen
Loosen my boots, love

lowse the flat oot
Aa'm ganna lowse the flat oot

create a commotion
I am going to create a commotion

lukka
Noo lukka!

look here
Now look here!

maak
He's a proper maak

maggot; mean person
He is very mean

maam
Aa'm gannin hyem to me maam

mum
I am going home to my mother

mad-het
Canny on, it's mad-het

very hot
Be careful, it is very hot

mair
Thor's nee mair bullets

more
There are no more sweets

man!

Give ower man!

an exclamatory term used when addressing either sex
Stop it man/woman!

28

mar
Howway, mar

friend
Come on, friend

marra
He's a marra o' mine at work

friend; workmate; colleague
He is a workmate of mine

mast
Haad on, the tea's not mast

brew
Hold on, the tea is not yet brewed

mazor
Wor Meggie's a mazor

amazing person
Our Margaret is amazing

meg
He's see mean he waad'nt gi' ye a meg

halfpenny
He is so mean he would not give you a halfpenny

Meggie
Wor Meggie

Margaret
Our Margaret

mek
Aa can mek nowt on't

make
I can make nothing of it

mekkin'gyem
Howway, but yor mekkin' gyem?

making game/fun
Come on, you are making fun?

mekkin' the sparks flee
If them two meet they'll be mekkin' the sparks flee

causing excitement
If those two meet there will be some excitement

mell
Cloot it wiv a mell

sledgehammer
Strike it with a sledgehammer

mesell
Aa've dyun it mesell

myself
I have done it myself

mettor
Whaat's a mettor?

matter
What is the matter?

mevvies
Mevvies Aa will an' mevvies Aa winnit

maybe
Maybe I will and maybe I will not

mind
Do ye mind aad Dode?

remember
Do you remember old George?

mind
Aa hev a mind to larn Jarmin

intention
It is my intention to learn German

29

min't
Haad on a min't

minute
Hold on a minute

missy-coo

Missy-coo!

miss it (sporting, or rather, unsporting)
Miss that putt!

Mistress
Hoo are ye gannin' on, Mistress Bell?

Mrs.
How are you getting on, Mrs. Bell

moont the cuddy
Howway, let we play moont the cuddy

children's game
Come on, let us play moont the cuddy

mooth
He got a bat o' the mooth

mouth
He was struck in the mouth

moothy
He's a bit moothy

talkative
He is a bit talkative

morder
If Aa get a haad on him Aa'll morder him

murder
If I get hold of him I will murder him

mow
Haad on a mow

moment
Wait a moment

muggles
Aa'm ganna play muggles wi' Jonty

marbles
I am going to play marbles with John

mushells
Haddaway get's some mushells

mussels
Go and get me some mussels

myest
Aa've eaten myest on't

most
I have eaten most of it

myun
Is't a full myun the neet

moon
Is it a full moon tonight?

naack
(the pronunciation of the'ck' must be stopped in the back of the throat)
Aa hev nee choice but to say naack

no

I have no choice but to say no

neb
Keep yor neb oot on't

nose
Keep your nose out of it

nee
Thor's nee tetties

no
There are no potatoes

neet
It's a caad neet the neet

night
It is a cold night tonight

neithor tack nor tyest
It's got neithor tack nor tyest

tasteless
It is tasteless

nettie
Whee's o' the nettie?

lavatory
Who is in the lavatory?

Newcassel
Aa'm away to Newcassel

Newcastle
I am going to Newcastle

neybors
We've got canny neybors

neighbours
We have nice neighbours

nigh enyuf for pit wark
It's nowt startlin' but it's nigh enyuf for pit wark

adequate
It is not a good piece of work but it is adequate

nivvor
Aa've nivvor crossed the doors aal day

never
I have never left the house today

noo then
Noo then, Geordie

hello
Hello, George

not ower grand
Aa'm not ower grand the day

not too well
I am not too well today

not reet
Whey, he's not reet, man!

mentally unstable
Well, he is unstable!

not tied
Aa'm not tied to gan doon theor

not obliged
I am not obliged to go down there

not wise
She's not wise, man!

silly
She is silly!

nowt
Aa hae nowt left

nothing
I have nothing left

nowt
He's a glaky nowt

person of no consequence
He is a slow witted, inconsequential person

nowt startlin'
Aa thowt he was nowt startlin'

ordinary
I thought he was very ordinary

numb
He's numb, man!

stupid
He is stupid!

31

nyeck'd
Aa was aal nyeck'd

naked
I was naked

nyuk
Sit doon i' the nyuk

corner
Sit down in the corner

oilin' he's wig
He's far ower fond o' oilin he's wig

drinking
He is very fond of drinking

on
Whaat's it myed on?

of
What is it made of?

on bank

Eftor he got hort iv a faal he got a job on bank

a colliery job on the surface rather than underground
After he was hurt in a roof fall he got a surface job

on't
Aa've nivvor hord on't

of it
I have never heard of it

ony
Hae ye ony aad claes?

any
Have you any old clothes?

oor
It'll tyek aboot an oor

hour
It will take about an hour

oot
She's oot at the toon

out
She is out at Newcastle

oot-back
Aa'm gannin' oot-back

outside lavatory
I am going to the lavatory

oot-bye
Aa'm gannin' oot-bye for some fresh air

outside
I am going outside for some fresh air

oot on't
Get oot on't as syun as ye can

out of it
Get out of it as soon as you can

oppen
Is't oppen?

open
Is it open?

orly
The orly bord catches the woorm

early
The early bird catches the worm

orth
Wi good orth ye can graa owt

earth
With good earth you can grow anything

ower
Aa'm gannin' ower to Gyetsid

over
I am going over to Gateshead

ower the wettor

He's woorkin' ower the wettor

over the River Tyne; overseas
He is working in Durham / Northumberland

owld
Aa'm ower owld for'd

old
I am too old for it

owld standards
The owld standards'll be tornin' i' thor graves

people of the recent past
The old people will be turning in their graves

owt
Is thor owt fresh?

anything
Is there anything new?

owt mair
Is thor owt mair?

anything else
Is there anything else?

paaky

He's a paaky bairn

choosy about food; no appetite
The child does not eat much

paan-shop
Aa'll hae to gan to the paan-shop agyen

pawn-shop
I will have to go to the pawn-shop again

paid oot
Aa'm paid oot

worn out; tired
I am tired out

pains
The poor aad sowl's crippled wi the pains

arthritis, rheumatism
The poor old soul is crippled with arthritis

pallatic

He got he'ssell pallatic i' the toon

extreme state of drunkenness
He got himself extremely drunk in Newcastle

panhacketty
Aa like nowt bettor than Panhacketty

meal using left-over meat
I like nothing more than Panhacketty

pay
Divvint fight him 'cos he'll pay ye

beat
Do not fight him because he will beat you

pease puddin

a pudding eaten hot or cold made from ham-flavoured split peas

pitmatic

the mining community version of the Geordie dialect

He taaks pitmatic

He uses the mining dialect

pittle
Haddaway an' pittle aback o' thon tree

urinate
Go and urinate behind tree

pity aboot ye

an expression indicating lack of concern

Pity aboot ye!

So what?

pit-yakkor

uncomplimentary description of a pitman

Whey, he's nowt but a pit-yakkor

Well, he is nothing but crude pitman

plank
Plank it doon heor

place
Place it down here

plissint
He's a varry plissint chep

pleasant
He is a very pleasant man

ploat
He got he'ssell a real ploatin'

pluck
He got himself plucked clean

plodgin'
He's plodgin' aboot lukkin for craabs

paddling in the sea
He is paddling about looking for crabs

pluff
Pluff it into yor snottercloot

spit
Spit it into your hankie

pollis
Gan an' get the pollis

policeman
Go and get the policeman

poother
Hae ye ony Beecham's poothers?

powder
Have you any Beecham's powders?

postin'
Aa've just seen the pollis postin' doon the raa theor

walking briskly
I have just seen the policeman walking briskly down the lane there

powny
He likes a bet o' the pownies

pony; horse
He likes a bet on the horses

prog
Prog a hole in't

poke
Poke a hole in it

pund
Len's a pund whey?

pound
Lend me a pound then?

puttin' in caad
She's puttin' in caad noo, mar

getting cold
It is getting cold now, mate

put yorsel away
Howway, ye'll hae to put yorsel away noo

get stuck in
Come on, you will have to get stuck in now

pyel
Ye'll just hae to pittle i' the pyel

pail
You will just have to urinate in the pail

pyeppor
Whaat's i' the day's pyeppor?

paper
What is in today's paper?

pyet
A baaldy pyet

head
A bald head

paid oot

raa
This is a lang raa

street; lane
This is a long street

rattle hor i' gannin'
Whey hinny, ye rattled hor i' gannin'

energetic, forceful action
Well mate, you hit that golf ball very hard

reed
Reed an' blue myeks porple

red
Red and blue makes purple

reet
Aa'm reet an' yor wrang

right
I am right and you are wrong

reglor
He's a reglor chorchgannor

regular
He is a regular churchgoer

35

rive
Rive it oppen

tear
Tear it open

rolly
He was knocked doon biv a rolly

lorry
He was knocked down by a lorry

roond the doors
Aa'm gannin' for a waak roond the doors

in the vicinity
I am going for a short walk

rowl
Rowl ower an' gi's a bit mair bed

roll
Roll over and give me more room in bed

rowled doon
Aa've rowled doon an' brokken me airm

fallen down
I have fallen down and broken my arm

saasa
Divvin' put yor tab ash i' the sassa

saucer
Do not put your cigarette ash in the saucer

sackless
He's far ower sackless

dozy
He is far too dozy

sair
Me airm's aaful sair

sore
My arm is awfully sore

sandas
Hae ye got yor sandas wi ye?

plimsolls
Do you have your plimsolls with you?

sands
Aa'm tyekkin' the bairn to the sands

the beach
I am taking the little one to the beach

Santy
Hae ye gettin' owt nice from Santy?

Santa
Have you had anything nice from Santa?

sartin
Are ye sartin he's gyen hyem?

certain
Are you certain he has gone home?

scaad
Be canny wi' thon kettle or ye'll scaad yorsell

scald
Be careful with that kettle or you will scald yourself

scraanchum
Gi's a bit o' scraanchum

The hard skin on roast pork
Give me a bit of the hard skin

scrafflin'

searching for something with a sweeping movement of the hand

Whaat are ye scrafflin' aboot eftor?

What are you searching for?

scrush
Scrush yorsell in

crush; force
Force yourself in

seam
He's iv a canny seam theor

situation
He is in a good situation there

see
Aa've nivvor seen him see baad

so
I have never seen him so ill

selt
He selt him a champion cuddy

sold
He sold him an excellent horse

set ye hyem
Howway hinny, Aa'll set ye hyem

take you home
Come on love, I will take you home

sharp
Ye'll hae to get up sharp the morn

early
You will have to rise early in the morning

shem
Whey, it's an aaful shem

shame
Well, it is an awful shame

shift
Wheor's me woork shift?

shirt
Where is my work shirt?

shoot
Thors nee need to shoot

shout
There is no need to shout

shows
We'll gan to the shows the day

the fair
We will go to the fair today

shuggyboats
Howway, Aa'll tyek ye on the shuggyboats

swingboats at the fair
Come on, I will take you on the swingboats

shul
Divvint lean o' yor shul, get on wi'd

shovel
Do not lean on your shovel, get on with it

shullin
Hae ye got a shullin' speor?

shilling (5p)
Do you have a spare 5p?

singin' hinnies
Aa love the smell o' singin' hinnies byekkin'

Northumbrian Scones
I love the smell of Northumbrian scones baking

sipe
Ye'll hae to sipe it oot wiv a tube

syphon
You will have to syphon it out with a tube

skeets
Me skeets is worn oot

boots
My boots are worn out

skelp
He wants he's hintend skelpin'

spank
He needs to have his backside spanked

skew-wiff
Yor claes is aal skew-wiff

uneven; untidy
Your clothes are untidy

skittors
He's i' the netty wi' the skittors

diarrhoea
He is in the lavatory with diarrhoea

skyet-gob
Noo listen, skyet-gob

fish-face
Now listen, fish-face

skyul
The bairn's gyen to skyul

school
The little one has gone to school

slavvor
Give ower slavvorin' aboot

saliva; aimless person
Pull yourself together

38

slee
He's far ower slee

sly
He is much too sly

sleep the caalor
Aa waarned he's slept the caalor agyen

to sleep in
I suppose he has slept in again

slop
Waatch oot, heor's a slop

policeman
Watch out, here is a policeman

slowsh
Gi's a slowsh o' yor pop

drink
Give me a drink of your pop

smaa'
He's just a smaa' chep

small
He is just a small person

smitt
Ye've gi'n is the smitt

virus infection
You have given me your cold

snaa
The snaa's caad

snow
The snow is cold

snammy
Aa love a bit o' raa snammy

turnip
I love a bit of raw turnip

sneck
Aa'll leave the door off the sneck

door latch
I will leave the door off the latch

sneck
Keep yor sneck oot on't

nose
Keep your nose out of it

snoot
He's elwis pokin' he's snoot inti'd

snout; nose
He is always poking his nose into it

snotter-cloot
Hae ye got a clean snotter-cloot?

handkerchief
Do you have a clean handkerchief?

soond
Divvin' myek a soond

sound
Do not make a sound

sowl
Thor waasn't a sowl aboot

soul
There was not a soul about

sowldger
The Jarmin sowldgers

soldier
The German soldiers

sowt
Hae ye sowt for'd?

sought
Have you sought for it?

spelk
Aa've gettin a spelk i' me hand

small sliver of wood
I have a spelk in my hand

spelk
Thor's nee need to be afear'd on a spelk like him

small lightly built person
There is no need to be frightened of a small person like him

spoot
Thor's a spuggy i' the wettor spoot

spout
There is a sparrow in the water spout

spuggy
Lukka the spuggies

sparrow
Look at the sparrows

spyun
Whee's got the sugar spyun?

spoon
Who has the sugar spoon?

squitts
Noo wor squitts

quits
Now we are quits

starvation
It's starvation oot there

extreme cold
It is extremely cold out there

starvin'
Let's get agyen the fire, Aa'm starvin'

freezing
Let me in beside the fire, I am freezing

stob
Tie yor gallowa to the stob

post
Tie your horse to the post

stoor
Howway, get aal this stoor cleared

dust; mess
Come on, clean up this mess

stop he's tap
Aa'll syun stop he's tap

call a halt to his activities
I will soon stop that

stott
The rain's stottin' off the roof

bounce
The rain is bouncing off the roof

stottie-kyek

Aa'll myek dee wiv a bit o' stottie-kyek

a large flat Northumbrian bun
I will make do with a bit of stottie-kyek

stottin' aboot
Aa seen him stottin' aboot oot-bye

falling about through an excess of drink
I saw him falling about outside

stowed-off
It's stowed-off in-bye

full
It's full inside

straa
A maan o' straa

straw
A man of straw

streyte
An' myek sure ye come streyte hyem

straight
And make sure you come straight home

stroonge
Be canny wi'm, he's varry stroonge

strange and menacing
Be careful of him, he is very strange

stumor
He's a right stumor

a person difficult to handle
He is beyond control

styebble
The cuddy's i' the styebble

stable
The horse is in the stable

styen
Whee hoyed that styen?

stone
Who threw that stone?

styffe
Ye canna get yor breeth for the styffe

fumes
You cannot breath for the fumes

styal
Sit doon o' the styul

stool
Sit down on the stool

summick
Summick to dee wi'd

something
Something to do with it

swaap
Aa'll swaap ye this gully for them muggles

swop
I will swop you this knife for those marbles

swallie
Swallie it off an' Aa'll get some mair

swallow
Swallow it down and I'll get some more

sweer
It's enyuf to myek a chep sweer

swear
It is enough to make a man swear

syreens
Aa mind the syreens i' the waar

sirens
I remember the sirens in the war

towsher

syun
Aa'll syun fettle thon up

soon
I will soon fix that up

taad
Dee whaat yor taad

told
Do what you are told

taa-taa
Howway son, we'll gan for a taa-taa

a walk with a child
Come on son, we will go for a little walk

tab
Hae ye got a tab?

cigarette
Do you have a cigarette ?

taffee
This is claggy taffee

toffee
This is sticky toffee

tally-maan
Aa need haaf-a-croon for the tally maan

credit draper
I need 2/6d (12½ p) for the credit draper

tee
Are ye gannin' tee?

too
Are you going too?

telt
He was telt

told
He was told

tettie
Gan an' howk a few tetties

potato
Go and dig up a few potatoes

the laads
Hoo did the laads dee?

Newcastle footballers
How did Newcastle get on?

the morn
Whaat are ye deein' the morn

tomorrow
What are you doing tomorrow?

the morn-neet
Aa'll see ye the morn-neet

tomorrow night
I will see you tomorrow night

the neet
Aa'm gannin' ti the toon the neet

tonight
I am going to Newcastle tonight

42

theor
Neithor heor nor theor

there
Neither here nor there

the reckly
Aa'll be wi ye the reckly

directly
I will be with you directly

the store
Haddaway to the store for some tea

the Co-op
Go to the Co-op for some tea

the toon
He's i' the toon

Newcastle
He is in Newcastle

thon
Divvin' worry aboot thon

that
Do not worry about that

thonder
The gissies is ower thonder

there
The pigs are over there

thor
Whaat aboot thor marras?

their
What about their friends?

thor
Thor ganna get tyun ower

they are
They are going to be taken over

thorsells
Let them see ti'd thorsells

themselves
Let them see to it themselves

thowt
Aa thowt nowt aboot thon

thought
I thought nothing of that

ti
Hae ye seen ti thon?

to
Have you seen to that?

tice
He was ticed inti'd?

entice
He was enticed into it

ti'd
Aa've seen ti'd

to it
I have seen to it

tiv
He kept it tiv he'ssell

to
He kept it to himself

tool
Wipe the clarts off wi' this tool

towel
Wipe off the mud with this towel

touched
The poor aad sowl's a bit touched

simple
The poor old soul is a bit simple

towe
Yor faather'll towe ye when he gets hyem

thrash
Your father will thrash you when he gets home

towld
It's whaat wor lass was towld

told
It is what my wife was told

towsher
He's a proper towsher

scruffy person
He is a really scruffy man

towsin'
The laads got an aaful towsin' last neet

decisive defeat
Newcastle United were hammered last night

trash
Gannin' up thonder's an aaful trash

exhausting journey
Going up there is very exhausting

tret
I was tret varry weel

treated
I was treated very well

tun wheyte
How! This is a tun wheyte!

very heavy
Here! This is very heavy!

twank
Gi'd a good twank

spank; strike
Strike it hard

tyebble
Tyek yor byuts off the tyebble

table
Take your boots off the table

tyek
Tyek it oot-bye

take
Take it outside

tyekkin' the wettor in
The laads is tyekkin' the wettor in

losing confidence
Newcastle are losing confidence

tyest
Aa divvin' like the tyest

taste
I do not like the taste

tyun
He's tyun baad

taken
He was taken ill

tyun
Gi wi a tyun

tune
Give us a tune

tyun ahaad
Hes the fire tyun ahaad?

taken hold
Has the fire taken hold?

tyun in
Aa've been tyun in wi this waatch

taken in
I have been taken in with this watch

understrapper
Tyek nee notice o' him,
he's nowt but an
understrapper

underling
Ignore him, he is just an
underling

up-a-heyght
Hoy the baal up-a-heyght

up in the air
Throw the ball up in the air

vally
Thor's nee vally in'

value
There is no value in it

varnigh
It's varnigh lowse

nearly
It's nearly closing time

varry
Aa'll varry syun be dyun

very
I will be finished very soon

varry canny
He's keepin' varry canny

alright
He is keeping alright

Waad
Waad yee di'd?

would
Would you do it ?

waadn't care but
Aa waadn't care but dee
away ti the toon

inclined
I am inclined to have a trip
to Newcastle

waal
Lowp ower the waal

wall
Jump over the wall

warse
It's gettin' warse insteed o'
bettor

worse
It is getting worse instead
of better

wedge
Aa'll wedge ye if ye divvin'
dee whaat yor telt

thrash
I will thrash you if you do
not do what you are told

weel
Aa divvin' feel varry weel

well
I do not feel very well

weel oiled
He was weel oiled when Aa
seen him

the worse for drink
He was pretty drunk when I
saw him

welt
Gi'd good welt wi yor No. 1 iron

lash
Lash into it with your No.1 iron

wesh
Haddaway an' wesh yorsell

wash
Go and wash yourself

wettor
Gi's a sup wettor

water
Give me a drink of water

whaat
Whaat di yee dee?

what
What do you do?

whaat fettle?
Noo then Geordie, whaat fettle?

how are you?
Hello George, how are you?

whee
Whee's thon?

who
Who is that?

whey
Aalreet whey?

then
Alright then?

whey
Whey, Aa think Aa'll dee away

well
Well, I think I will go now

whey aye
Whey aye Aa'm reet!

of course; definitely
Of course I am right!

whey it's likely
Are they ganna lose the neet? Whey it's likely!

definitely
Are they going to lose tonight? Definitely!

whey ye buggor mar!
Whey ye buggor mar! It's wor bairn

expression of delight
Well I never! Our son has returned

whisht
Whisht, Aa thowt Aa hard summick

be quiet
Be quiet, I thought I heard something

wi
Wi'll hae to be gannin'

us; we
We will have to be going

wi
Are ye gannin' wi wi?

with
Are you going with us?

wi'd
Whaat are ye ganna dee wi'd?

with it
What are you going to do with it?

willicks
He's oot gettin' willicks

winkles
He is out collecting winkles

willie-waft
Aa could dee wiv a good willie-waft

drink
I could do with a pint

winna
He winna dee whaat he's telt

will not
He will not do what he is told

winnit
She winnit di'd

will not
She will not do it

wiv
Wiv aal o' wi

with
With all of us

woork a flankor
He tried ti woork a flankor but he was fund oot

outflank; trick
He tried to trick them but was found out

wor
Wor aal paid oot

we are
We are all exhausted

wor
Wor bairn's not clivvor

our
Our child is not well

wor laad
Wor laad's gyen oot

my brother
My brother has gone out

wor lass
Wor lass is bonny an' baad

my wife
My wife is very ill

worsells
Wor gannin' worsells

ourselves
We are going ourselves

wrang
Two wrangs divvin' myek a reet

wrong
Two wrongs do not make a right

yammor
Give ower yammorin'

incessant whining talk
Stop whining

yark
Aa'll yark yor hintend

hard blow
I will give you a hard blow on the rear

yelhoose

yee
Whaat are yee deein'?

you
What are you doing?

yel
Aa could dee wiv a pint o' yel

ale
I could do with a pint of ale

yelhoose
He's roond i' the yelhoose

public house
He is round at the pub

yep
He's a proper little yep

ape; monkey
He is a proper little monkey

yett
Put the sneck o' the yett

gate
Put the latch on the gate

yit
Aa'm not dyun yit

yet
I am not finished yet

yorsell
Divvin' fash yorsell

yourself
Do not worry yourself